D1312770

Team Strings 2

An integrated course for individual, group and mixed instrument teaching

Violin

Richard Duckett, Olive Goodborn & Christopher Rogers

International
MUSIC
Publications

Published by
International Music Publications Ltd
Griffin House 161 Hammersmith Road London England W6 8BS

Edited by BARRIE CARSON TURNER

Piano accompaniments by BARRIE CARSON TURNER

Sincere thanks are extended to the following people:
CHRISTOPHER BULL, author and arranger of ensemble TEAM STRINGS BOOK 1, for the original plan for TEAM STRINGS BOOK 2.
CELIA DOUBLEDAY, cellist, who worked on the material in preparation.
ANN GOODBORN, double bass tutor who worked with Christopher Bull on ideas for the original draft.
MONICA HERMOLLE, cellist, for her invaluable support in the preparation of these books.
BRIAN LESTER, Birmingham Instrumental Team, for his invaluable advise and support.
SHELAGH REID, violinist and teacher (Aberdeen), for her invaluable advise on technical matters and repertoire.
JENNY SMITH, violinist and teacher (Worcestershire), for her invaluable advise and support.
LORNA WINDASS, violinist and teacher (Addenburgh, Oxfordshire), for her invaluable support and help on bowing the material.

First published 2002

Music engraving and typesetting: Barnes Music Engraving Ltd, East Sussex TN34 1HA

Contents and CD Track listing

	Track	Page
Violin tuning tones	1	-
Viola tuning tones	2	-
Abschied	23	28
Acapulco Bay	33	44
Au Clair De La Lune	32	43
Auld Lang Syne	42	58
Believe Me, If All Those Endearing Young Charms	31	41
Blowin' In The Wind	40	53
Camptown Races	28	36
Caribbean Dance	38	49
Country Gardens	22	27
Coventry Carol	45	61
Daisy Bell	5	5
Eternal Father	49	65
Heigh-Ho	4	4
Hoe Down	43	59
I Got Rhythm	19	24
I Know The Lord's Laid His Hand On Me	37	48
I Saw Three Ships	17	22
Joy To The World	18	23
Little Donkey	39	51
Liza Jane	36	47
Loch Lomond	15	21
Lullaby	34	45
Lullaby (Brahms)	14	19
Marie's Wedding	29	38
My Bonnie Lies Over The Ocean	6	7
My Grandfather's Clock	3	2
My Heart Will Go On	48	64
New World Symphony	11	18
O Little Town Of Bethlehem	35	46
Oh! Susannah	27	34
Oh, Lady Be Good!	25	32
Over The Rainbow	24	30
Pink Panther	50	66
Sailor's Song	10	17
Scotland The Brave	16	21
Shortnin' Bread	41	56
Soldier, Soldier	7	10
Star Wars	47	62
Summertime	46	61
Swing Low, Sweet Chariot	13	19
Take It Away Man	9	15
The Girl I Left Behind Me	30	39
The Rowan Tree	12	19
The Teddy Bears' Picnic	21	27
The Truth From Above	44	60
This Train	8	14
Waltz From The Merry Widow	26	34
When The Saints Go Marching In	20	25

Team Strings 2 Ensemble

TEAM STRINGS 2 ensemble material has been specially written so that it can be played by almost any combination of string instruments the teacher may encounter.

On each ensemble page there are three or four parts. The first is the melody and the second is a duet part. The third and fourth parts are either a bass line, a harmony part or a descant. Each piece can therefore be used as a solo, duet, trio, or quartet with or without piano accompaniment.

By allocating the parts to different instruments it is easy to create a considerable variety of mixed ensembles, from a simple duet to a full string orchestra.

Each piece which can be played in emsemble or with a piano accompaniment also has the option of a CD backing track.

In addition to this, each piece can be extended into a longer one by varying the textures in subsequent verses. This can be done by reallocating the parts, playing in unison, using pizzicato accompaniments, introducing solo passages, etc.

The following symbols have been used to provide an immediate visual identification:

  Pieces with piano accompaniment

  Ensemble page
(score included in ACCOMPANIMENTS book)

  Pieces which appear in the same place on the same page in all four TEAM STRINGS 2 books

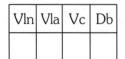

Vln	Vla	Vc	Db

The box to the left of each arrangement or score indicates where each piece can be found in the solo instrumental books.

Introducing Team Strings 2

As in TEAM STRINGS, TEAM STRINGS 2 has been designed to meet the needs of young string players everywhere, whether lessons are given individually, in groups or in the classroom.

Musical variety

TEAM STRINGS 2 has been specially designed to follow the original TEAM STRINGS TUTOR, although it can be used to follow on from any beginner string book. It offers the same wide variety of musical styles as the original, but is further enhanced by titles from the world of jazz and blues supported by a three-part course of improvisation techniques.

Ensemble pieces

TEAM STRINGS 2 offers corresponding pages of music which can be played in harmony for mixed string ensembles, from duet right up to full string orchestra. From page 43 onwards, TEAM STRINGS 2, TEAM BRASS, PERCUSSION and WOODWIND naturally share much of the same ensemble material allowing it to develop into full orchestra. As the TEAM STRINGS 2 tutors contain 25 pages of ensemble, they are suitable for school orchestra, string orchestra, symphony orchestra as well as solo, duet and other small groups.

Flexible course

TEAM STRINGS 2 does not offer guidance on how to play or teach a string instrument but rather offers material which the professional teacher can use to structure courses for individual pupils.

National Curriculum & GCSE skills

TEAM STRINGS 2 has been designed to help meet the requirements of the National Curriculum for music. In addition to fostering musical literacy, 'Play By Ear' lines provide early opportunities for composition and improvisation. This aspect of TEAM STRINGS can be a useful starting point for these elements in the GCSE examination course now followed by secondary schools.

Comprehensive notes on the use of this series, scores of the ensemble material, piano accompaniments and approaches to creative music making are given in the accompaniments book.

Accompaniments

Accompaniments for selected solo pieces, and the ensemble pieces, are available in the Accompaniments book and on the CD.

Lesson diary and practice chart

Date (week commencing)	Enter number of minutes practised							Teacher indicates which pages to study
	Mon	Tue	Wed	Thu	Fri	Sat	Sun	

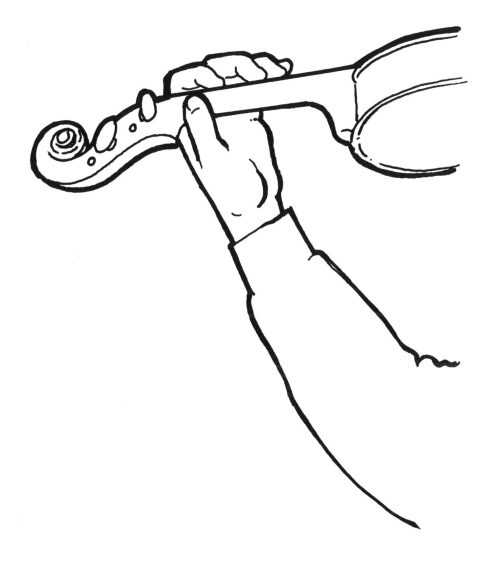

My grandfather's clock

Words and Music by
HENRY CLAY WORK (1832–1884)

4 clicks intro

The four dots mean
you can repeat the music
as often as you want

Moderately

3.

Moderately

4.

* Chime effect. Repeat chord 12 times, ad lib., and hold.

4

Heigh-ho

7 clicks intro

Words by LARRY MORLEY
Music by FRANK E. CHURCHILL

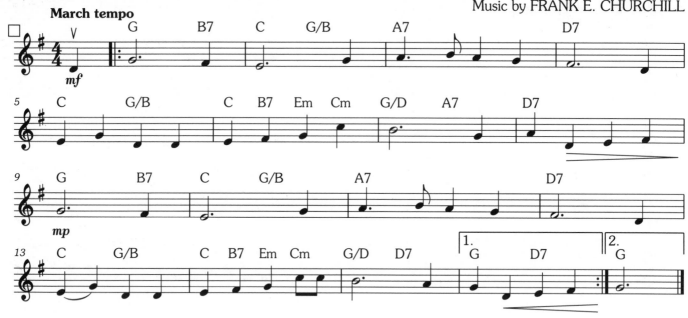

Simple gifts

Shaker melody

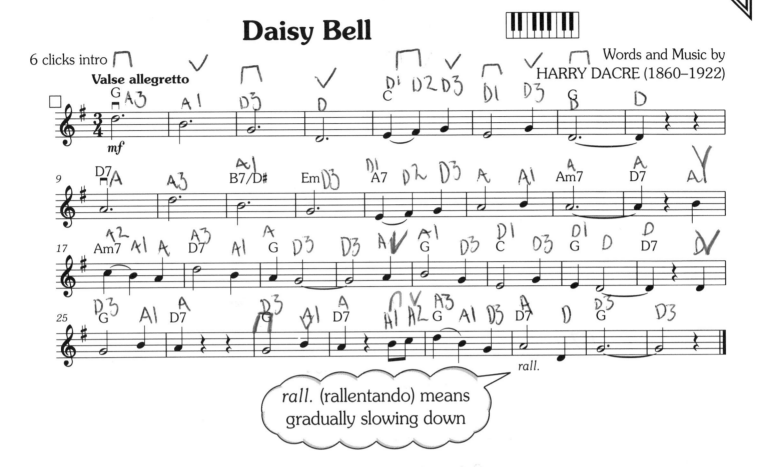

If you're happy and you know it

Oranges and lemons

The Lincolnshire poacher

Traditional

Slur study

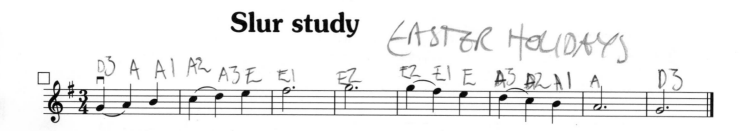

Key signature of E minor

Melancholia

CHRISTOPHER BULL (1950–1994)

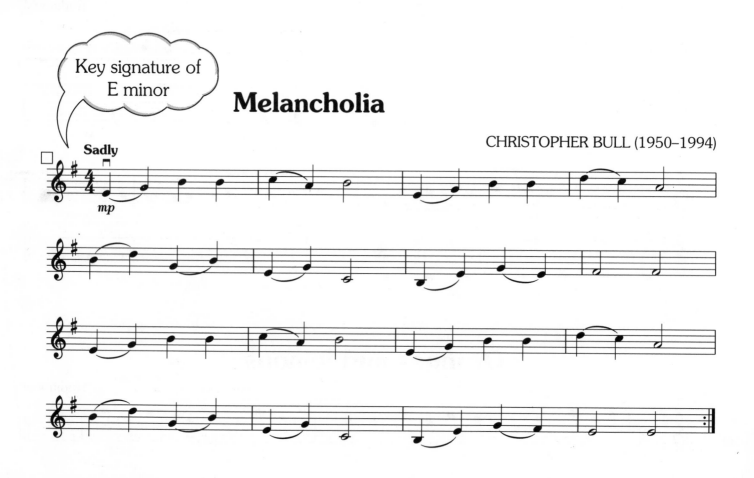

My Bonnie lies over the ocean

5 clicks intro

Traditional

Staccato

Legato
means play the notes smoothly

Staccato
means play the notes short

Etude 1

Etude 2

Staccato duet

CHRISTOPHER BULL (1950–1994)

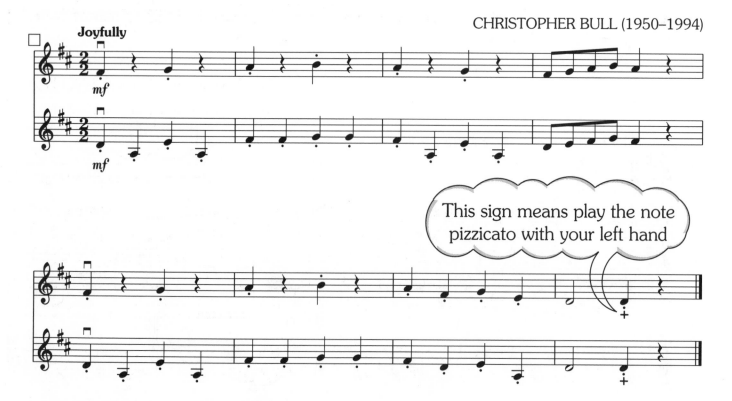

This sign means play the note pizzicato with your left hand

West Heath lilt

The cuckoo

EDWARD DUCKETT

Hornpipe

HENRY PURCELL (1659–1695)

Soldier, soldier

4 clicks intro

Traditional

Broken slurs

Das Blumchen wunderhold

LUDWIG VAN BEETHOVEN (1770–1827)

Sleigh ride

CHRISTOPHER BULL (1950–1994)

Study 1

German tune

Traditional

Study 2

Minuet in G

HENRY PURCELL (1659–1695)

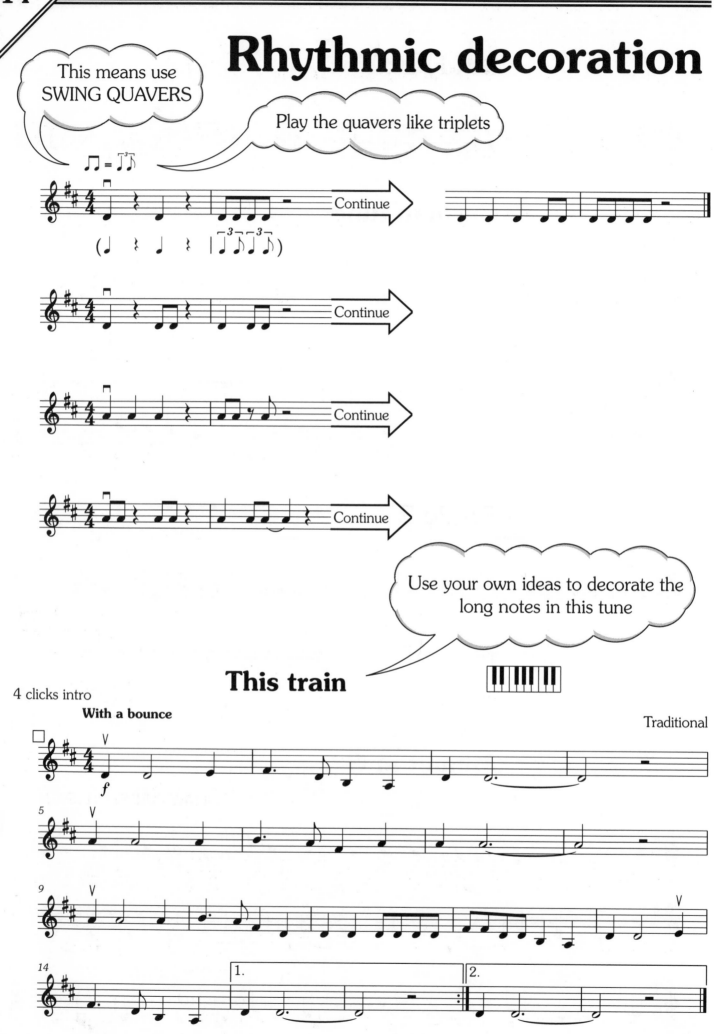

Take it away man

4 clicks intro

Cockles and mussels

Traditional

Hoch Wass' kommt von draussen Rhein

Traditional

With a gentle rhythm

Fairly fast

Sailors' song

4 clicks intro

Traditional

The key of D major

Music in D major has a
key signature of TWO sharps

L. A. nitespot

Twelve bar blues

Lasst uns erfreuen

Chorale melody

New world symphony

4 clicks intro

ANTONIN DVOŘÁK (1841–1904)

The rowan tree

3 clicks intro

Traditional

rit.

Swing low, sweet chariot

4 clicks intro

Traditional

Lullaby

5 clicks intro

JOHANNES BRAHMS (1833–1897)

For (s)he's a jolly good fellow

Comin' thro' the rye

Traditional

Snappily

Loch Lomond

Traditional

3 clicks intro

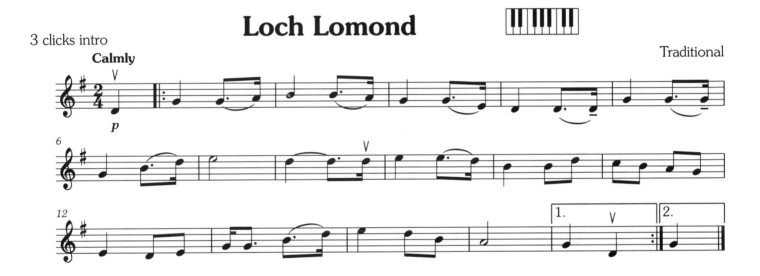

Scotland the brave

4 clicks intro

Traditional

Moderato

Continue

I saw three ships

4 ♩. clicks intro

Traditional

Joy to the world

4 clicks intro

GEORGE FREDERIC HANDEL (1685–1759)

1.

2.

3.

Melodic improvisation

IMPROVISATION means you make up your own music or answer another player's phrase

Continue these tunes by adding a 2-bar answering phrase

I got rhythm

4 clicks intro

Music and Lyrics by
GEORGE GERSHWIN and IRA GERSHWIN

Use the notes in the box for your improvisation

When the saints go marching in

5 clicks intro

Traditional

Medium swing

1.

After playing the tune you can
IMPROVISE over parts 2, 3 and 4

Medium swing

2.

Medium swing

3.

Medium swing

4.

The key of C major

Music in C major has a
key signature of no sharps or flats

Observe the rests if
playing with viola or cello

Scale and arpeggio of C major

Biddy Biddy

Easy tempo

Traditional

Look for scale
patterns

Round the scale

This means rest for 3 whole bars, so count ①2, ②2, ③2 and then play from bar 4

The teddy bears' picnic

JOHN W. BRATTON

Country gardens

4 clicks intro

Traditional

Summer is icumen in

Round

Traditional

Abschied

6 clicks intro

Traditional

Intervals

Study in C

Steadily

Fine

D.C. al Fine
slower

Over the rainbow

4 clicks intro

Moderately

Words by E. Y. HARBURG
Music by HAROLD ARLEN

Harmonics

Touch the notes lightly with the 4th finger to play the harmonics

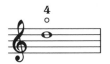
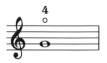

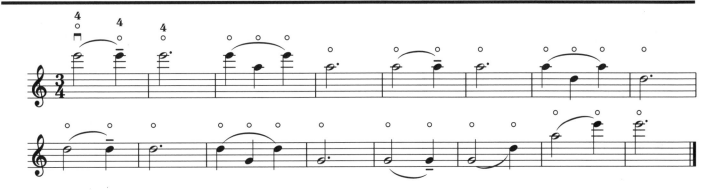

Pearls

Wistfully

Using the 4th finger

The keys of Canterbury

Traditional

Oh, how lovely is the evening

Round

Traditional

Polovtsian dance

ALEXANDER BORODIN (1833–1887)

Barn dance

Waltz from The Merry Widow

6 clicks intro

FRANZ LEHÁR (1870–1948)

Oh! Susannah

4 clicks intro

STEPHEN C. FOSTER (1826–1864)

Scale and arpeggio of G major
(2 octaves)

Etude 1

Etude 2

Soliloquy

Camptown races

STEPHEN C. FOSTER (1826–1864)

4 clicks intro

Lively

mf

COL LEGNO means tap the strings
with the wood of the bow

Hickory, dickory, dock!

Traditional

Steadily

mf

Col legno

mf

Black Forest

Fits with *German Tune* in book 1, page 23

Summer's end

Fits with *Autumn* in book 1, page 21

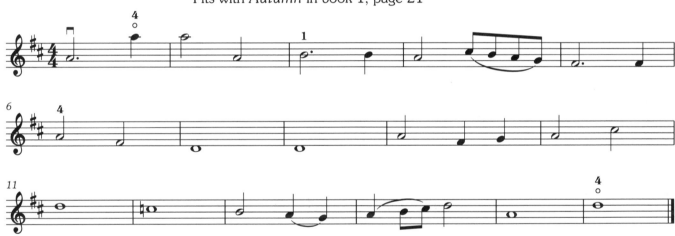

Caribbean carnival

Fits with *Jamaican dance* in book 1, page 49

High B

Marie's wedding

4 clicks intro

Cindy

The girl I left behind me

4 clicks intro

Traditional

The northern lights of old Aberdeen

MARY WEBB

Hot cross buns

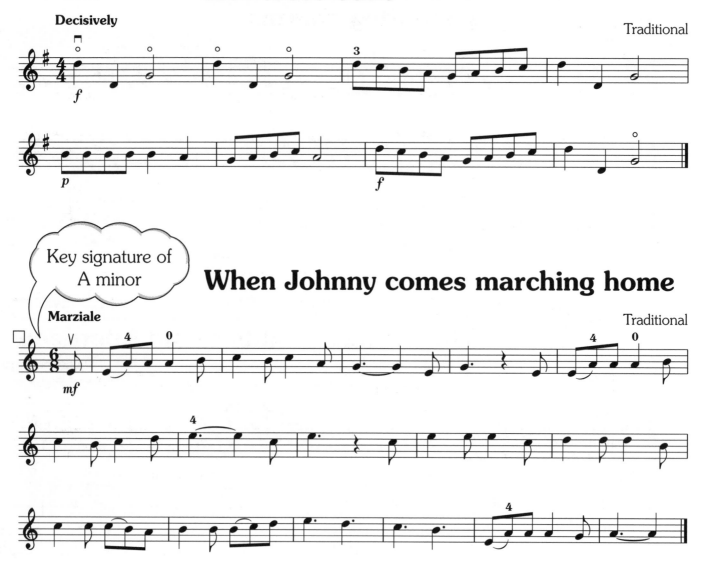

When Johnny comes marching home

God save the Queen

Believe me, if all those endearing charms

THOMAS MOORE (1779–1852)

5 ♪ clicks intro

The key of F major

The note B♭

Music in F major has a key signature of ONE flat

The FLAT lowers the pitch of a note by one semitone

Barcarolle

JACQUES OFFENBACH (1819–1880)

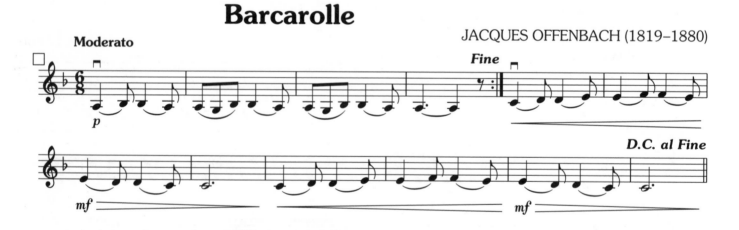

Slow waltz

Triste

Make up your own tunes using the notes G, A, B♭, C and D

Edelweiss

Words by OSCAR HAMMERSTEIN II
Music by RICHARD RODGERS

Au clair de la lune

Fits with *Au clair de la lune* in Brass,
Woodwind and Percussion books (page 37)

Traditional

4 clicks intro

Upper B♭

Acapulco Bay

4 clicks intro

Fits with *Acapulco Bay* in Flute and Oboe books (pages 6 and 7)

Tempo de beguine

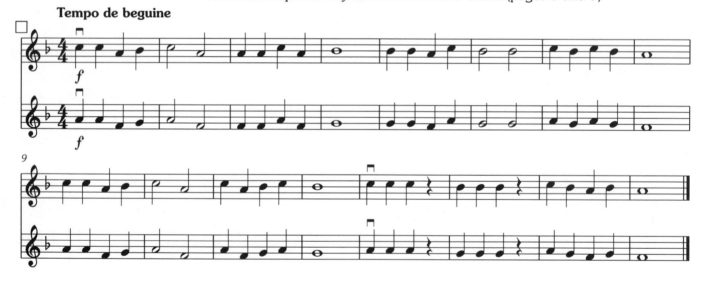

Slur round

Steady

Fits with *Step round* in Flute and Oboe books (page 8)

Skip to my Lou

Playfully

Traditional

Lullaby

Fits with *Lullaby* in Brass, Woodwind and Percussion books (page 14)

6 clicks intro

O little town of Bethlehem

Fits with *O little town of Bethlehem* in Brass, Woodwind and Percussion books (page 49)

This melody can also be used with the accompaniment part in Team Strings book 1 (page 45)

3 clicks intro

Traditional

Upper F

Scale and arpeggio of F major

Little boy blue

Traditional

Fight the good fight

JOHN L. HATTON (1808–1886)

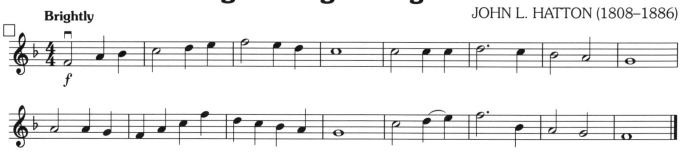

Liza Jane

4 clicks intro

Traditional

Pentatonic improvisation

Question and answer

Using the pentatonic scale on D

I know the Lord's laid his hands on me

7 clicks intro

Traditional

Caribbean dance

7 clicks intro

Traditional

The key of B♭ major

The notes E♭ and Upper E♭

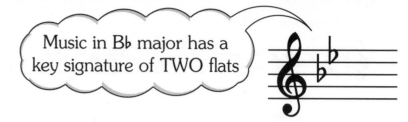

Music in B♭ major has a key signature of TWO flats

(4)

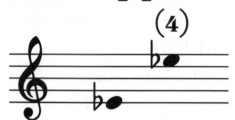

Scale and arpeggio of B♭ major (low)

John Brown's body

Marziale

Traditional

mf

Scale and arpeggio of B♭ major (high)

 ## Little donkey

Fits with *Little donkey* in Brass, Woodwind and Percussion books (page 37)

Words and Music by ERIC BOSWELL

4 clicks intro

Pomp and circumstance

EDWARD ELGAR (1857–1934)

Blowin' in the wind

Fits with *Blowin' in the wind* in Brass, Woodwind and Percussion books (page 21)

Words and Music by BOB DYLAN

4 clicks intro

Third position

The magic carpet

Fits with *The wizard* in Team Strings book 1 (page 43)

Etude

The notes high C#
and high D

High C#

High D

Pease pudding hot

Traditional

Moderately

mf

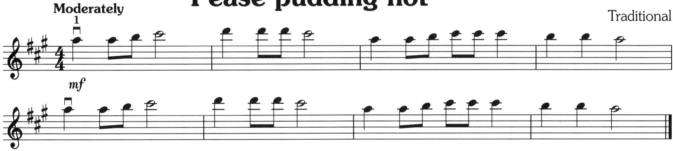

Scale and arpeggio of D major (2 octaves)

Song and dance

Fits with *Song and dance* in Team Strings book 1 (page 26)

Bright and rhythmic

Traditional

The key of A major

Music in A major has a
key signature of THREE sharps

Low C♯

Row, row, row the boat

Round

Flowing

Traditional

Shortnin' bread

4 clicks intro

Traditional

The note G♯

Scale and arpeggio of A major
(2 octaves)

All made up

Moderately

Victorian ballad

Slow waltz tempo

Auld lang syne

4 clicks intro

Traditional

1.

2.

3.

Hoe down

4 clicks intro

Molly Wicks and the pupils
of Greenmeadow Junior School

divisi

1.

2.

3.

Key signature of D minor

Scale and arpeggio of D minor harmonic
(2 octaves)

D minor round

The truth from above

3 clicks intro

Traditional

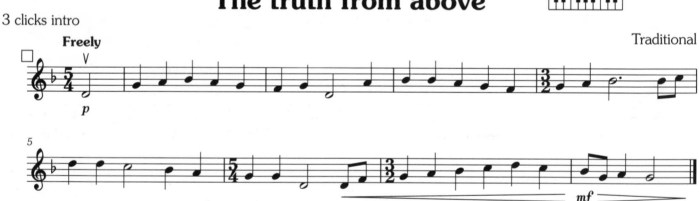

Charlie is my darling

Traditional

Scale and arpeggio of G minor harmonic
(2 octaves)

Key signature of G minor

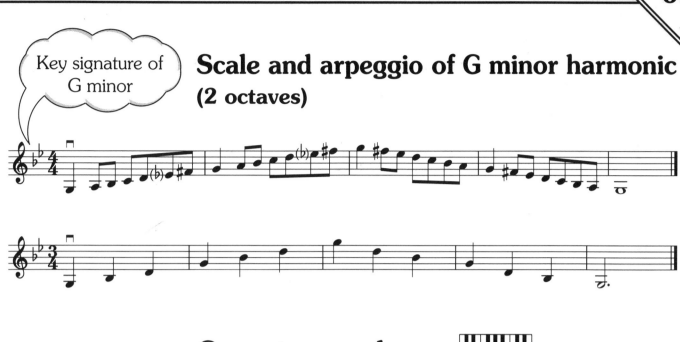

Coventry carol

3 clicks intro

Traditional

Moderately

Summertime

6 clicks intro

Music and Lyrics by GEORGE GERSHWIN, DUBOSE and
DOROTHY HEYWARD and IRA GERSHWIN

Moderately, with expression

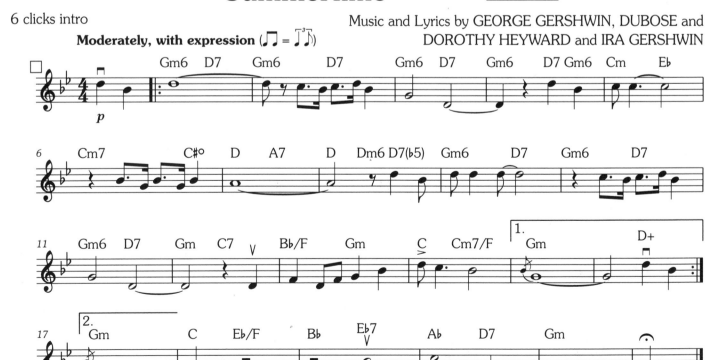

Star wars

4 clicks intro

JOHN WILLIAMS

My heart will go on

Love theme from *Titanic*

Words by W. JENNINGS
Music by JAMES HORNER

4 clicks intro

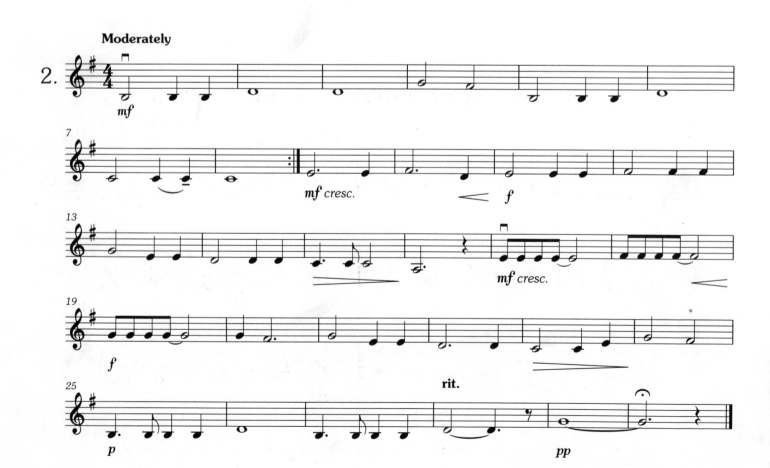

3.

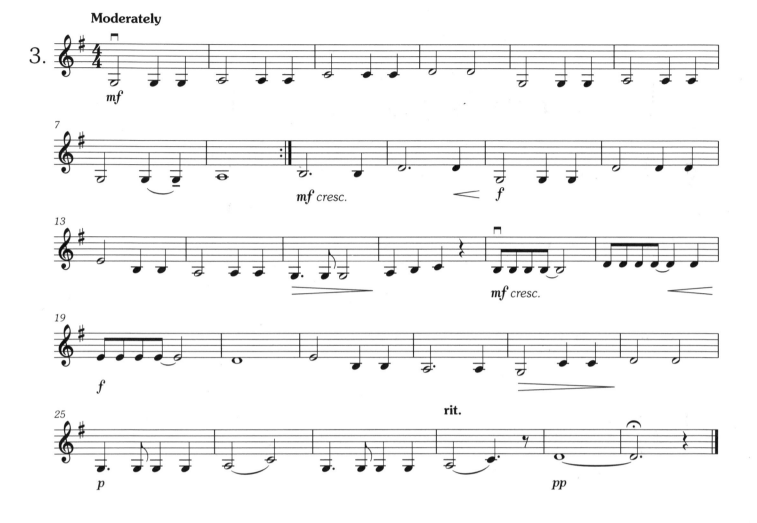

Eternal Father, strong to save

Words by W. WHITING
Music by J.B. DYKES (1823–1876)

3 clicks intro

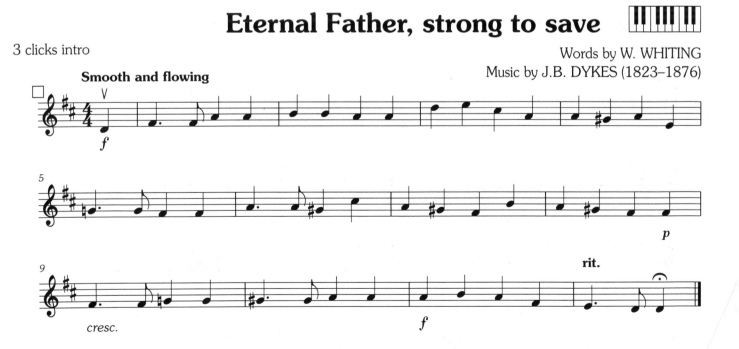

Pink Panther

7 clicks intro

HENRY MANCINI

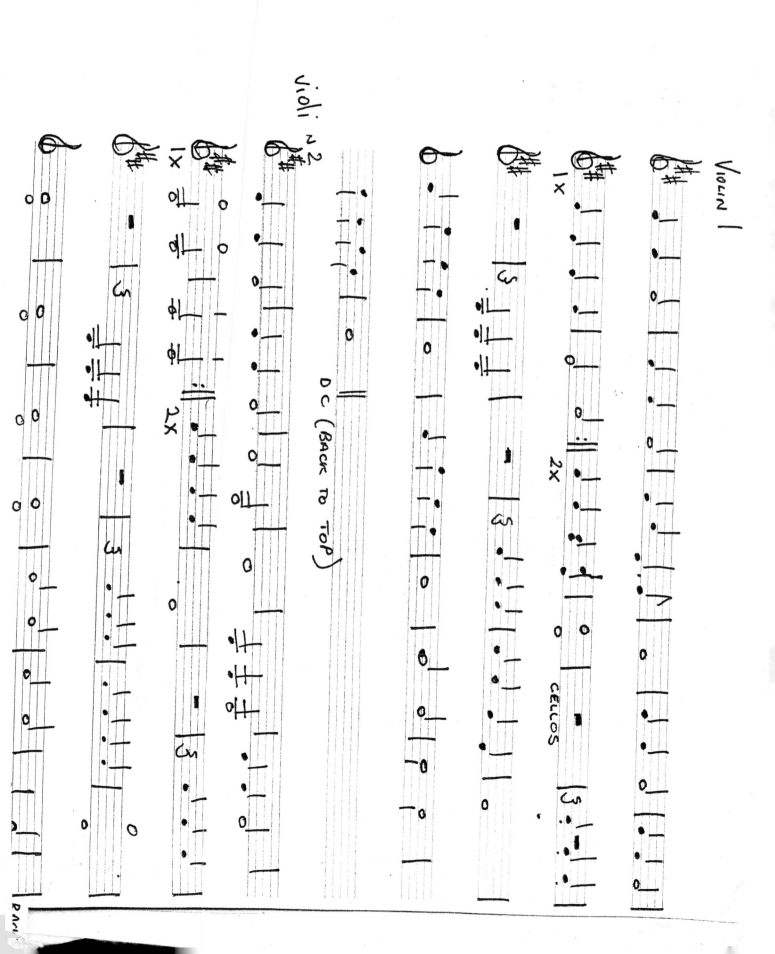